NOW—FOR THE FIRST TIME BETWEEN COVERS—BESTSELLING

BOOKS IN SUPERCONDENSED FORM! WHY WASTE TIME

READING A WHOLE TOME WHEN YOU ONLY NEED A FEW

PAGES TO MAKE CONVERSATION?

THIS BOOK IS DESIGNED TO MAKE YOU THE LIFE OF YOUR

NEXT PARTY, AND IT WON'T STRAIN YOUR BUDGET OR YOUR

SHOULDER WHEN YOU CARRY IT IN YOUR BEACH BAG. ENJOY!

THE 7 HABITS OF HIGHLY DEFECTIVE PEOPLE

AND OTHER BESTSELLERS THAT WON'T GO AWAY

A PARODY

Cathy Crimmins and Tom Maeder

DOVE
BOOKS

ISBN 0-7871-0748-4

Printed in the United States of America

Dove Books
8955 Beverly Boulevard
Los Angeles, CA 90048

Distributed by Penguin USA

Text design and layout by Stanley S. Drate/Folio Graphics Co. Inc.
Cover design and layout by Rick Penn-Kraus
Interior Illustration by Wesla Weller

First Printing: September 1996

10   9   8   7   6   5   4   3   2   1

The Best of the Bestseller List

Fiction

THE FRIDGES OF MARIN COUNTY
by Robert "Fats" Waller
A hip California housewife finds brief happiness in the arms of an Iowa refrigerator repairman.

THE BESTSELLING PROPHECY
by Jimmybob Bluefield
A seeker of truth goes to Chile to find platitudes.

THE FARM by John Grasschopper
A young doctor becomes suspicious when he gets his dream job at a Midwestern organic farming conglomerate.

Biography, Autobiography, and Personal Narrative

TIM AND ELLEN AND ROSEANNE AND JERRY as told to Norman Mailer
The ultimate sitcom celebrity gang-bang autobiography.

EMBARRASSED BY THE LIGHT
by Etta Beady Eye
A guide for people who are self-conscious about near-death experiences.

A YEAR IN POMPEII by Peter Magma
Fond pre-Vesuvius anecdotes and recollections.

HAVING OUR LAY by Sadie and Bessie Delicious as told to Jo Hill Hearth
Memoirs of the world's oldest sexually active sisters.

IRON TOM: HELPING YOUR NEUTERED CAT REGAIN HIS MASCULINITY by Robertson Bly
A celebration of purring in the belly for he-cats everywhere.

General Nonfiction and Other Psychobabble

THE "YOU'RE HOT, BABY" ZONE
by Sturges Preston
A deadly flesh-eating virus affects Hollywood agents.

THE BELLBOTTOM CURVE
by Richard J. Armani and Charles Mizrahi
A study reveals the connection between class, intelligence, and sartorial style.

LISTENING TO PRINGLES by Peter D. Kracker, grocer, Ph.D.
A psychologist/grocer chronicles his experience in treating depressive patients with prescription junk food.

HOW WE FLY by Sherman Newlin, M.D.
A doctor's brief and fruitless exploration of the impossible.

REVIVING OEDIPUS by Sophocles Smith, Ph.D., and Cassandra Medea
Observations on troubled adolescent boys.

Self-Help and How-to

NINE STUPID THINGS WOMEN DO TO MESS UP THEIR CLOTHES by Laura Samsonite
Tips on preserving the dignity of your wardrobe.

THE SEVEN HABITS OF HIGHLY DEFECTIVE PEOPLE by Steven I. Covet
Nose picking and other annoying strategies for getting what you want.

WINDOWS FOR DUMBBELLS
The complete guide to low-tech fenestration.

MARS AND VENUS IN THE BATHROOM . . . AND ALL AROUND THE HOUSE
by John Spalding Green
They're at it again, those zany gender-impaired lovers!

And Bear in Mind . . . Other Bestsellers

INTERVIEW WITH AN UMPIRE by Anne Brown Rice

THE CHEESEDOODLE REPORT by Charity Cheesedoodle

WAITING TO EXHALE THROUGH THE HIDDEN SENSES OF LUCK by Sunny Tan Macmillan

"S" IS FOR SUPERCALIFRAGILISTICEXPEALODOCIOUS by Sue Graphite

THE CAT WHO COUGHED UP A HAIRBALL by Lillian Jackson Browne

EAT JUNK AND LIVE MINUTES LONGER by Sixpak ChoppedLiver

YOU KNOW YOU GOTTA STOP LAPDANCING WHEN HIS BELLY GETS TOO BIG
by Erma LaBomba

WOMEN WHO RUN WITH THE MALLRATS by Clarissa Benetton

MEDITATIONS FOR WOMEN WHO DON'T DO A DAMN THING by Ida LaMoment

SMART WOMEN, FOOLISH INVOICES by Lucretia Mint, CPA

PLAY MYST FOR ME by Clint Westwood

POLITICALLY CORRECT MEIN KAMPF by Huckleberry Finn Garner

JURASSIC PORK by Michael Cretin

AN EVEN BRIEFER HISTORY OF TIME by Stephen W. Hookah

THE PHYSICIAN'S DESK REFERENCE

THE HORSE'S ASS by Stephen J. Glued

THE HUNT FOR BLUE NOVEMBER by Tom Fancy

CONTENTS

The Fridges of Marin County

ROBERT "FATS" WALLER

The Beginning

There are songs that gibber and babble up the wazoo and down the drain. This is one of them. Last spring, I sat in my study staring into space when the telephone beckoned.

The caller was a former Marin County resident. He now seeks nirvana in Tibet. He had a story to tell. Did I want to hear it?

I agreed to meet him in San Francisco for coffee the following day. His willingness to travel so far on a moment's notice impressed, but did not surprise me. People will do anything for attention.

Over decaf cappuccino he spun an interminable, tedious, superfluous yarn about his mom. He showed me warranties, service receipts, and a rambling journal kept by his old lady, Fresca, who boffed a repairman.

I made him return seven, eight times to America, just for fun. Would I tell the story? Yes, I said. What a hoot. Would I treat his tale with respect? Sure thing, bud. There's one born every minute.

Robert Kitchenaid

On May 12, 1978, the Acme Appliance Company dispatched Robert Kitchenaid to Marin County, California. He hoisted six boxes of tools and spare parts into his truck, Blanche. Acme wanted to prove durability. Seven of the earliest Acme refrigerators, the AR-1000, pink and aerodynamic, made in 1955, still functioned there. Some West Coast decorator with a fifties fixation thought they were great accessories. "Have a look at 'em," Acme told Kitchenaid, seeing possible PR opportunities.

As a child Robert liked to tinker. Later he joined the army, became a machinist. Came to know, love, and fix equipment. When the war ended, he drifted into appliance repair. Refrigerators were always his favorite—their large, manly bulk; their hard, warm exterior; their bright, cool insides. Refrigeration symbolized man's triumph over the vicissitudes of temperature and spoilage.

His wife had left him years before. He understood. Everyone understood. Why wouldn't she?

Robert Kitchenaid had strange habits. He smelled bad. He was obese. He was dumb.

Fresca Jackson

F resca sat by the pool on her enormous estate sipping the very best wine in the world. An acquaintance bought it for $1 million and gave it to Fresca on a whim. Life was good.

Fresca was rich, brilliant, beautiful, and successful. She was CEO of a *Fortune* 500 company. Her third symphony had opened at Carnegie Hall. The watercolors she painted during an evening art class were snatched up by galleries and sold for a fortune. With the proceeds, Fresca built shelters for widows and orphans.

Her husband was handsome, witty, and charming. Their marriage was sublime.

Then Robert Kitchenaid arrived.

> **ROBERT KITCHENAID**
> **APPLIANCE REPAIR**
> **WINTERSET, IOWA**

The plain black lettering on his battered panel truck impressed her. It was so different from the ornate service vehicles in Marin County, where every carpenter was a former aerospace engineer, every plumber a Nobel laureate gone bad.

" 'Fresca'—I like a woman named after a soft drink," Robert Kitchenaid said. "So bubbly!"

Sinatra crooned on the truck radio. Kitchenaid's uniform was immaculately pressed and starched. He had sewn the company's logo patch on by himself with neat, compulsively regular stitches. When it came to work, he was perfect. Otherwise he was a slob.

"Show me your fridge, ma'am?" said Robert Kitchenaid. His belly and butt drooped over his belt and jiggled as he talked. A thin line of drool seeped from the left corner of his mouth. Fresca gazed at him in awe. He affected her profoundly. She was accustomed to tight, young, beautiful bodies, not this.

Prime Time, Fast Food

During their four days together, Robert Kitchenaid showed Fresca life. He cleaned and reorganized her refrigerator. He taught her to adjust the thermostat so that ice cream would not melt, lettuce would never freeze. "Defrost regularly," he said in his dreamy way, wisdom born of dusty roads in far-off lands.

They made Bundt cake together, clipped coupons, cooked snacks whose recipes were found on package sides. In the evening, he changed into a gray sweat suit and old running shoes. He sprawled before her television, belching, scratching, scarfing down snacks.

"Slim Jim?" he offered. Her teeth ripping at the jerked meat made her feel crude, bestial. When washed down with Kool-Aid, it evoked thoughts of death and the jungle.

A Roll in the Hay

*S*ex with Robert Kitchenaid was terrible. Fresca's husband always made love to *her slowly, through long delicious evenings that lasted till morning. With Robert it was just wham-bam-thank-you-ma'am. Then he rolled over to sleep or flipped on the TV. It made her feel as women had not felt since the fifties—since the days of her big, pink refrigerator.*

"Robert, all my life I have felt profound feelings and thought complex thoughts. You trivialize everything. With you my life seems so simple. For the first time I feel shallow, ridiculous!"

"Huh?" muttered Robert, watching basketball on TV.

Gobbets

Forty years later, a birthday mug of liquid nutrients in her hand, Fresca drove her motorized wheelchair into the kitchen. This was where they had stood. She sighed and thought back over every second of their days together, one second at a time. The refrigerator was still there, long silent in spite of Acme's dream.

She reread, for the trillionth time, the letter the law firm sent her ten years ago. "In accordance with his last wishes, the remains of Robert Kitchenaid were chopped into gobbets and put down an Acme Model GR-6000 garbage disposal. He asked us to send you his receipt book, his sweat suit, and the remote control from his TV."

Fresca opened the refrigerator door, as she had so many times before. The same food was neatly arranged as he left it. She had watched it go from fresh to rancid to moldy to mummified. *Such is the passage of our lives*, she thought. It had been good, she said to herself, and fell over dead.

Windows for Dumbbells

How to Use This Book

How to Use This Book

Read it.

How This Book Is Organized

It starts at the beginning, proceeds through the middle, and stops at the end. Page numbers are expressed in positive integers, which occur sequentially. The covers are on the outside, the pages on the inside. The top of the book should be held upward, the bottom down.

Help

There are no help functions in books. You must buy *Help for Dumbbells 7.5*. To use that program, refer to the book *Help for Help for Dumbbells 7.5*.

Icons Used in This Book

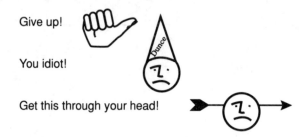

Give up!

You idiot!

Get this through your head!

What Are Windows?

What Are Windows?

Windows are a high-resolution, full-color, user-friendly, silica-based multimedia interface between the user and outdoor non-virtual reality.

How Do J Install Windows?

Cut a hole in the wall and fasten them in.

Calibrating the size of Windows to the size of the hole is important, as no simple "Make Fit" functions are available.

What Do Windows Do?

They open. They close. They let in light. They allow you to see out without letting in cold, heat, or bugs.

What Are Screens?

What Are Screens?

Screens are debugging filtering matrices used together with the Open Windows function.

Where Do I Find Screens?

Screens are generally available at hardware, home supply, or specialty Windows stores.

What Are Screen Savers?

Screen savers are usually not necessary, regardless of what the store clerks might say. As long as you do not lean on screens and avoid poking lit cigarettes or sharp objects through them, they can last for many years with minimal maintenance.

Windows Commands

What Are the Commands?

Windows use simple pull-up and pull-down menus. Pull up and they open. Pull down and they close.

These instructions apply only to Double-Hung Windows. Casement, jalousie, and other specialty Windows use different operating systems with their own sets of commands. (See *Casement Windows for Dumbbells*, *Jalousie Windows for Dumbbells*, etc.) Many modern offices use nonopening or "hermetically sealed" Windows that require "bricks" (see *Bricks for Dumbbells*), "rocks" (see *Rocks for Dumbbells*), or other data management accessories for opening (see *Other Data Management Accessories for Dumbbells*).

Troubleshooting

Finding Lost Windows

Windows are not lost even during power surges or shortages.

If you lose Windows, you were probably drunk and wandered into a closet by mistake.

When Windows Crash

When heavy data is rapidly entered into Windows, the system may crash. In this case, the entire silica chip or "pane" must be replaced.

Exiting Windows

Exiting Windows, or "defenestration," is an emergency bailout procedure developed by financial data specialists during the 1929 stock market crash.

To exit Windows, first open Windows, then open Screens (if not already open). You have now created an empty space. Enter.

If you wish to leave a note, remember to write and save it before exiting Windows.

THE "YOU'RE HOT, BABY" ZONE

A Terrifying True Story of a Deadly Virus That Ate Hollywood Agents

STURGES PRESTON

SPECIAL PREFACE TO THE PAPERBACK EDITION:

To the Reader:

This book is nonfiction, and, boy, am I peeved. The story is true, and the agents mentioned here are real. That's why they held up the movie deal and Dustin Hoffman made *Outbreak* instead. Now I'll never get a script optioned from my book and that deal for the Burger King tie-in toys is lost forever.

Sure, I constructed the dialogue in the book from actual conversations with Hollywood agents whose flesh was being devoured by man-eating microbes during our interviews together. I know I shouldn't have chuckled as I watched them writhe in agony, but how was I to know that they would take it so personally? My wife had already gone shopping for her Oscar gown, and now we're in counseling.

So thanks for buying this paperback edition—it's my only hope for big bucks, unless I miraculously find another cool (or hot!) disease that eats away at another hated sector of society like, say, lawyers, or meter maids. But what are the odds of that?

STURGES PRESTON

ICM/CAA
INFECTIOUS AREA

No authorized entry except for food delivery and Federal Express pickup

To open this door,
place ID card on sensor
or tell us a personal fact about Michael Ovitz.

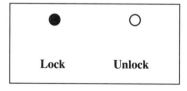

PROCESSING . . .

You are clear to enter (or proceed—
enter is rather phallic, don't you think?) . . .

SUITE AA-5

INVESTIGATOR:
Col. Tonya Harding

AGENTS IN USE:
Evian, Calistoga, Unknown

Proceed forward.

BIOSAFETY LEVEL

0

LOCKER ROOM

STATUS:
Female, no breast implants (yet)

Remove EVERYTHING touching the skin: clothing, rings, contact lenses, etc.
Change into sterile surgical scrubs and split-crotch panties—whoops—

You are cleared to enter . . .

BIOSAFETY LEVEL

2

CAUTION:
Ultraviolet Light.
Please wear at least SPF 15.

BIOSAFETY LEVEL

3

Staging Area/Rehearsal in Progress

ALARMS:

Enabled on all fifty Porsches in parking lot.

SPACE SUIT STATUS:

Ready. Wonderbra insert available.

CAUTION

BIOHAZARD

BIOSAFETY LEVEL

$$\boxed{4}$$

**AIR-LOCK DOOR/DECON SHOWER/ANTILOCK BRAKES
DO NOT ENTER WITHOUT WEARING SPACE SUIT**

ID code please?

You are cleared to enter . . .

. . . but we have run out of paper for this paperback edition of *The "You're Hot, Baby" Zone*. Hope you enjoyed the signage, and watch for Sturges Preston's new book, *Danger Signs All Around the World.*

THE
BESTSELLING
PROPHECY

JIMMYBOB BLUEFIELD

One day my old girlfriend, Boopsie, telephoned and asked me to meet her at the airport. We hadn't spoken in twenty-three years, but why not?

We sat in the lounge. She looked great, just as I remembered. At least I thought I remembered. Suddenly I was not sure that I had ever known her at all.

"Fred," she said, "I got this fortune cookie the other day. I thought of you, a credulous loser with lots of spare time and money to burn who's willing to pursue anything. This fortune may be the secret to everything, a fragment of the Supreme Fortune Cookie. I wanted to let you in on the ground floor."

GO SOMEPLACE. YOU WILL LEARN SOMETHING, the cookie read. That was enough for me.

She said, "Oh, by the way, Fred, 'A stitch in time saves nine.' "

I felt that I was embarking on a great quest.

The next scheduled international flight was headed for Chile. What a coincidence, I thought. The beer I had in the lounge with Boopsie was chilly. I went.

The nonstop flight to Chile gave me much insight. As we climbed to thirty-six thousand feet, objects on the ground grew smaller. The terrestrial world shrinks with distance.

The hostess offered light lunch: a Western omelette or spinach quiche, a salad, and a cookie. Cookies everywhere! A man twelve rows in front of me requested quiche. He ate the cookie. I moved up behind him and whispered through the crack between the seats, "Where are you going?"

"Chile."

Again a coincidence! What was the likelihood that he, of all 214 people on board, would be headed for the same destination?

"What do you know of cookies?" I asked.

"I know of the second platitude," he said. " 'THAT'S THE WAY THE COOKIE CRUMBLES.' " I felt that I was getting closer to the secrets of the universe. At some point during the night, this passenger was brutally murdered. At least I think he was: His eyes were closed and he did not move. It became clear that the government, or some strange power, was trying to suppress the Supreme Fortune Cookie.

I detected little green flying saucers following us through the air. I begged the stewardess to tell the pilot to shake them, but I could still see them when we reached our destination. I wore a hat made of vomit bags to keep those in the saucers from reading my mind. It worked.

At the Santiago airport, I went to the taxi stand. A taxi was waiting. Another coincidence.

"Hi, I'm Bil, and I'll be your driver today. Where do you want to go?"

"I'm looking for the Supreme Fortune Cookie. Are you?" I asked breathlessly.

Bil turned slowly and looked at me. "As long as the meter's running, pal, I'm looking for whatever you're looking for."

I felt the oneness of the world in my quest.

High in the Andes I encountered a drop-dead gorgeous broad who said, "Yo, pal, you look like a guy searching for the Supreme Fortune Cookie."

"I am," I said, after a pause.

She smiled at me. "The third platitude is this: 'WHAT GOES UP MUST COME DOWN.' "

"Are you a scholar?" I asked.

She said she had been an astrophysics professor at the University of Colorado, but this platitude was the most amazing thing she had ever heard.

She chuckled. "I dropped everything and came right down."

She explained to me that this Andes community was made up of empiricists as well as loonies. She led me to a field where forty young men and women carried out controlled tests of the platitudes. Half of them chucked rocks up in the air and watched to see if they came down. The other half threw rocks down toward the ground to see if they'd return upward.

Each result was carefully noted. After an infinite number of throws they would achieve certainty.

Sometimes the researchers put their heads over or under the flying rocks to determine whether this interposition of the rational human brain would alter the results. It did. At the end of two hours, the down-throwers all remained hard at work, while the up-chuckers, without exception, lay senseless on the rich South American soil. The results were conclusive: The brain stands between us and our pure understanding of the world.

I saw a young priest in flowing robes. "Are you looking for the Supreme Fortune Cookie?" I asked.

He looked at me thoughtfully. "You bet. Isn't everyone? But the nasty government keeps it a secret." He paused. "Have you communed with the aliens and vegetables yet?" he asked.

I thought for a moment. I had done many dumb things in my life, but not that. Not yet. "No," I said with a sigh.

"Push on your closed eyelids and tell me what you see," he said.

I saw crazy shapes and patterns. "I see crazy shapes and patterns," I said.

"Those are messages from other beings," he said.

"Why do I only see them when I push on my eyes?" I asked.

The priest grinned broadly. "That is the intergalactic sign for 'Talk to me!' "

I was awed again. "What are they saying?"

He smiled. "We are only beginning to understand. Three hundred people spend their days pressing on their eyeballs, learning how to translate."

The next morning Bil and I drove off on our quest for the Supreme Fortune Cookie. A man tripped and fell in the road. Bil ran over his legs. We got lost and drove around in circles. We came to a man with crushed legs lying in the road.

Bil hesitated a moment, then said, "I have seen a man like that before, only his legs were not so flat. What a coincidence."

The man gazed up at us. He, too, was in search of the Supreme Fortune Cookie. I could tell by his *SFC Quest '96* T-shirt. He said, " 'Don't cry over spilt milk.' 'Easy come, easy go.' 'It's always darkest before the dawn.' "

Hot damn! We had three more platitudes.

For ten days, Bil and I woke ourselves in the middle of the night, hoping to glimpse that extra darkness before the dawn. It just seemed to get lighter and lighter. During the days, we poured milk on the ground and resisted the temptation to weep.

The man, who had stayed with us, smiled gently. "Your milk is not the original milk. You have 1 percent, 2 percent, whole, skim, and Lactaid. Early milk was not locked up in bottles or cartons. It came straight from animals. It was free, and not homogenized or pasteurized."

In the market square of a small town the people milled about, eagerly exchanging platitudes. "A bird in the hand is worth two in the bush." "If you can't take the heat, get out of the kitchen." "Tippecanoe and Tyler, too." "When it rains it pours."

Men in uniforms arrived and shot sixteen people. Blood spattered on my face. Yuck. In that instant I realized the difference between living people, who stand up and breathe, and dead people, who lie down and don't. This was not the whole difference, but more knowledge would come.

I think I also glimpsed the entire story of life, from primordial soup through the ultimate future. I don't remember any details, but I'm sure I saw it, which makes me feel smug.

Two weeks later Bil, José, Pepe, and two priests sat with me in a tent. Four hundred thousand heavily armed troops massed outside, having come for the sole purpose of keeping me from the next platitude. Squadrons of fighters and bombers flew overhead. The trembling of the ground suggested that miners were tunneling underneath us.

José said with a grin, "I think that if we walk out very quickly and don't talk to them they will not see us."

We managed to escape.

We drove down the mountain. We saw a billboard: SUPREME FORTUNE COOKIE PLATITUDES, 10 MILES. Every mile there was another sign, the numbers diminishing one by one. Ten miles later, on the outskirts of a small town, stood a tent with a sign: SUPREME FORTUNE COOKIE PLATITUDES HERE. I entered.

A woman looked at me. "Hi, I'm Marjoram. You must be looking for information about the Supreme Fortune Cookie."

"How many platitudes are there?" I asked.

She smiled. " 'Birds of a feather flock together.' 'A rolling stone gathers no moss.' 'Nothing ventured, nothing gained.' "

I scratched my head. "Is that all?"

She smiled. "I've got a million of 'em. But we must be careful. The government will kill us all if they know what we're after."

I paused and pondered. "What *are* we after?"

Marjoram looked at me with disgust. "The purpose of the platitudes, of the Supreme Fortune Cookie, is to make people like you as shallow and foolish as possible. You are also psychotic, which is an added bonus."

"But the government is trying to stop this?" I asked after a moment.

She smiled at me. "Yes. Contrary to what many believe, governments were created by society for its own good. Government has the people's best interests in mind. The government wants people to be able to take care of themselves."

I thought about this for a minute.

She continued. "People like me, on the other hand, want to make lots of money off of credulous fools such as you, sap your energy, drain your mind of all originality and discernment. The platitudes turn you into imbeciles, sheep, who will buy self-help books, diet products, tapes by motivational speakers, and the like. We will turn you into intellectual vegetables."

"Is that good?" I asked.

She thought for a moment. "Well, it's organic."

I was having a hard time grasping this concept. "Will I become a better person?" I asked.

She laughed a deranged, hysterical laugh. "No, of course not. But no one really cares whether you're a better person, and in the end you won't know the difference. I, on the other hand, will accelerate the evolution of us few, turning us into rich and decadent authors living lives of indolent luxury in between bestsellers. Just us and the publishers. And one day we will do away with books, save the forests, abolish publishers, and sell you a bill of goods on-line while siphoning money directly out of your accounts."

I felt that I had finally achieved my goal. I was content.

She said, "Oh, hang on, sucker. I've got some more platitudes for you. But you'll have to buy the next book in the series to get them."

INFORMATION FROM THE AUTHOR

Send $20 or more in cash or money order to the author. Don't bother to include your name or address: I know who you are, I can see you looking at this page right now. In return you will embody the principle "A fool and his money are soon parted."

TIM *and* ELLEN *and* ROSEANNE *and* JERRY

or

Never Stand Too Close to a Naked Fat Lady
Making Your Point in Sein Language

as told to NORMAN MAILER

THE ULTIMATE CELEBRITY GANG-BANG AUTOBIOGRAPHY

Hi!

We're celebrities from TV sitcoms. Everyone knows we couldn't write a sentence if our lives depended on it, but we're bestselling authors anyway! How do we do it? We believe in the supernatural, at least when it comes to ghostwriters. They haunt us regularly. They sit around watching and listening while we berate our staff and fix our makeup. They hang on our every word—we spill our guts on tape and then, like literary cleaning ladies, these highly educated spirits dust our sentences and line them up nicely to be consumed by our adoring public.

You see, it's not enough to squeeze a lot of money out of you during our TV series, where your consumer dollars pay for those endless commercials. We want more. We want you to go to your local bookstore and buy stacks of our autobiographical masterpieces to give to your friends and family.

Recently, a bunch of us TV sitcom stars got together and realized that we could make even *more* money if we only employed *one* ghostwriter. And, if we went in on it together, we could get a really good, famous writer who would have to come out to L.A. and grovel and take notes and be generally humiliated.

So that's how this wonderful book is coming to you (just perfect for all those Moms, Dads, sisters, ex-wives, and crossing guards on your gift list!). We got together for an orgy of self-congratulation one long weekend in Malibu and offered Norman Mailer $3 million to be our scribe. Naturally, he's a fat old man who couldn't resist the invitation, and we're just tickled pink to have our wonderful selves represented in print by one of America's literary legends.

In this book, you'll find out things about us sitcom stars never before revealed to anyone, except maybe to *Entertainment Tonight* and a couple of the tonier tabloids:

- All of us—Roseanne, Tim, Jerry, and even Ellen, were abused prenatally, and we learned to cope with it by telling jokes to our imaginary fetal friend.

- Jerry says he would date Roseanne if only she were seventeen!

- Ellen and Roseanne want to adopt a baby, or, if possible, Ellen plans to be artificially inseminated with Paul Reiser's sperm to start a sitcom dynasty!

- Tim wears his tool belt even when he's naked!

- After four days of listening to us talk about ourselves, Norman Mailer said he preferred Gary Gilmore's company.

LISTENING TO PRINGLES

PETER D. KRACKER, grocer, Ph.D.

Toward the end of 1975, not long after the introduction of Pringles brand potato snacks, I had occasion to sell a cardboard tube of this novelty food to a melancholic customer. Sam, a short, greasy, pudgy, pasty, unattractive individual whose shopping hours betrayed a life undisturbed by a steady job or social life, had frequented my market for years. Junk food was clearly his means of dealing with the profound unhappiness in his life. During the late 1960s, Sam had used packaged cupcakes with chocolate icing. In 1971, he tried high doses of cheese curls during a six-month period, but was finally obliged to stop when his fingers, hair, and eyes turned orange. Twinkies, Ring Dings, beer nuts, popcorn, and a host of other snack items followed fast upon one another during the next few years. Each held initial promise; every one, in the end, left Sam in deeper despair.

I suggested potato chips to Sam. No one knows why the combination of potato, oil, and salt has such a beneficial effect on crazy people, but generations of Irish, German, French, and American researchers have empirically verified the effect. Medical and grocery science are often based on simple experience rather than theory. For a time, potato chips seemed to work: Sam grew more cheerful and began to think about the future. He spoke of changing careers (from what, I do not know), marrying, starting a family. He took up hobbies, such as weaving edible coverlets from pasta products and collecting torn paper bags from around the world. But gradually, as so often happens, the therapeutic benefit dwindled and vanished. Sam returned to his normal, morose self.

Pringles were a completely unprecedented concept in potato-based snacks. Their bipolar, saddle-shaped format physically corresponds to the up-and-down moods of junk-food fiends whose minds are often traumatized by repeated exposure to flat or irregular chips. Regular, nested shapes, on the other hand, provide soothing consistency for individuals whose lives otherwise lack this quality, while the cardboard container, unlike standard foil or cellophane bags, can be used in many arts and crafts projects at the loony bin.

Less than two months after I started Sam on Pringles, he successfully ran for city council. Within a year, he married, had three lovely children, and began a lucrative recording career in rock music. To my delight and surprise, the Pringle effect did not diminish over time. Though Sam's dose and precise flavor choice had to be modified from time to time—communion wafer Pringles during his tenure as Archbishop, Pringles with lithium chloride seasoning through the rough period when he was tried for the Nicole Simpson murder—he continued to flourish emotionally. Sam (not his real name) eventually won a Pulitzer Prize, won the Nobel Peace Prize, was elected president of the United States, and hosted the top-rated late-night TV talk show.

I am left with a haunting question. Is it right to use Pringles? Did I help Sam, or was there some more "real" and fundamental Sam, the non-Pringle Sam, the pathetic, destitute, suicidally depressed, ugly, lonely, boring, stupid Sam who should have been allowed to burden society with his ghastly destiny? What *is* one's true self? And how do we grocers best serve our customers?

HAVING OUR LAY

The Story of the World's Oldest Sexually Active Sisters

SADIE AND BESSIE DELICIOUS
as told to Jo Hill Hearth

69 weeks on the *New York Times* bestseller list!

Now a smash Broadway/Couch Dancing show!

PREFACE

The *New York Times* first assigned me to interview Sadie and Bessie Delicious in 1991—at the time, the sisters were the oldest living multicultural exotic dancers on 42nd Street. Sadie, now 111, and Bessie, 109, are of Swedish, Ethiopian, Japanese, Swiss, and French heritage. ''They're amazing,'' said their manager, Clyde Bungler. ''They appeal to guys of all ages. Why, I've even had some seventy-year-olds in here who get turned on by their feistiness.''

After I completed my article for the *Times*, the men of America fell in love with the Delicious Sisters. They wanted to know more about their lives and, specifically, their sexual histories. I've spent hours with Sadie and Bessie, organizing their pasties, cataloging their pinup shots, and going through their little black books to tell their story. It is a story of women unafraid to celebrate their sexuality, women unhampered by marriage or motherhood, women who fought hard to have a career when the world didn't always approve.

Note: Many men have tried to find the Delicious Sisters since my article first appeared. In particular, they want to know more about the ''lollipop stick'' technique they supposedly perfected in the 1920s. Because the sisters must guard their privacy and their income, they are unavailable to the unpaying public. However, if you can pay their fee of $2,000 per hour, they can be reached at 1-800-OLD-GALS.

A SAMPLING OF WIT AND WISDOM FROM THE COUNTRY'S MOST BELOVED SISTERS . . .

Why, I remember, when Bessie and me was in our teens, there was this little kid, Ben, and he paid us money to take off our clothes and play doctor with him. Yep—that Benjamin Spock was a commie liberal even back then.   *—Sadie*

Thomas Edison came by a lot to our Lulu Club up in Harlem. Sadie was quite taken with him, until she found out that he had hidden a movie camera in their room while they was doin' it. Whew! She chased that Tom Alva all around until he gave her the film!   *—Bessie*

I like that Heidi Fleiss. She's one young woman with gumption. She's got spunk!   *—Sadie*

I did Franklin Roosevelt, and Eleanor, and even little Fala, their dog. I liked being close to the First Family. I offered them a New Deal every time.   *—Bessie*

Houdini was a great guy. Of course, he liked to wear a straightjacket while we were doing it, but I didn't care.   *—Sadie*

You know, it used to be hard for us hookers before the Sexual Revolution. They called us Wicked Women and we got syphilis and we never got to go to the opera. Now we get to go to the opera.   *—Bessie*

C'mon, Hugh Grant! You'll never go back to Elizabeth Hurley when I get through with you. Did you ever have a woman with no teeth? —*Sadie*

Not many people know that Sadie and I were in the bunker with Adolf and Eva. It was one of those kinky things that most historians leave out. —*Bessie*

Milton Berle used to come by in his dress after his TV show. He taught me all I know about eye makeup. —*Sadie*

JFK wasn't all that great. Now, Harry Truman—there was one hunk of a man!

—*Bessie*

MARS AND VENUS IN THE BATHROOM
... AND ALL AROUND THE HOUSE

JOHN SPALDING GREEN

Meet Mars. He leaves the toilet seat up. Meet Venus. Her soggy Donna Karan knee-highs hit Mars in the face every time he steps into the shower. How can this cosmic couple harness their sexual identities to cope with toothpaste tubes, dripping lingerie, and leaky faucets? Is a man's technique for toilet plunging really more effective than his mate's, or can he tap into his feminine side and even get a crush on the Tidy Bowl man?

Meet me, John Spalding Green. Once I was a monk. We had no women. We had no bathrooms. I didn't know Mars and Venus from Abbott and Costello. And yet I persevered. I left the monastery, got myself a mail-order Ph.D. and a hot girlfriend, and within six weeks I knew everything there was to know about sexual relationships. First I identified Mars and Venus and put them in a book and on infomercials and audiocassettes. Then I followed them into the bedroom, where I analyzed all of their sexual habits.

But that wasn't enough, because Mars and Venus can't spend all day and night in bed. They have to go about their normal lives. And so I have created this series, which will help you understand how men and women are different in *every* environment.

The Mars and Venus Series.
Collect 'em all !!!!!!

- *Mars and Venus in the Closet.*
    How gender influences space considerations.
- *Mars and Venus at the Mall.*
    Including Mars's surreptitious visits to Victoria's Secret.
- *Mars and Venus at the Parent-Teacher Conference.*
    See how Mars recovers after forgetting their child's name and age.
- *Mars and Venus at the Car Dealership.*
    Miata or Mini-Van? Maybe we should stay planetary, buy a Saturn, and take The Road Less Traveled.
- *Mars and Venus in Their Entertainment Center.*
    Remote controls as sex substitutes and other issues.

EMBARRASSED
by the Light

ETTA BEADY EYE

*T*here I was, a perfectly ordinary middle-American woman—a bit of a glutton. One day at the county fair, I stuffed a huge bite of weenie into my mouth, and the next thing I knew I was choking, gasping for the breath that never came, writhing, falling, with faces swimming all about me. Then I was dead.

I looked down from on high and saw my own body, slumped repulsively between the weenie stand and the ringtoss, with little cotton candy–smeared urchins clustered 'round saying, "Eeeeew, she's all blue, mommy!" Suddenly my life came into perspective. It sucked. I felt a great sadness sweep over me.

Sadness that my life had been so lousy. Sad that I was dead. Sad that I had left so many things undone, like finishing that weenie. One thing about the world beyond: If you're hungry when you get there, you stay hungry for a long time.

Just then a choir of celestial angels rushed up to me, singing and dancing. Among them I could see Elvis, and the Big Bopper, and Glenn Miller, and Ricky Nelson. Even Frank Sinatra made a preview appearance. And great painters stood around creating fabulous masterpieces, like Leonardo da Vinci and Andrew Wyeth and Norman Rockwell. The great poets of all time—I forget their names, but they were *great*—spontaneously made up odes and limericks and hexameters and micrometers about me.

I felt so humble, what with all the great beings of all time—no, everyone who had ever lived, every *creature* that had ever lived, every *plant* and microbe, even the stones and stars, the angels and God Him/Her/It-self gathering about to welcome and praise and adore me. "All this?" I wondered. "For me?" Somewhere in the back of my dead mind a voice murmured, "No, you idiot! You're just insane! You forgot to take your medication this morning!" But I dismissed this voice, because doubts and uncertainty get us nowhere.

The spirits of Andrew Carnegie, John D. Rockefeller, Croesus, King Midas, P.T. Barnum, and Al Capone appeared before me and said, in unison, with four-part harmony, "Your time has not yet come. You should not be here. You still have work to do on earth."

"What?" I asked. What could little old me possibly do that these rich white dead guys could not?

So they told me. There is, they said, a fortune to be made peddling afterlife nonsense to gullible dumbbells. "You will write a book," they said, "and appear on television and radio, conduct seminars. You will rake the bucks in hand over fist." All they asked in return was 25% of the take, deposited in a secret account in a Tibetan bank.

It sounded good to me, so I got a dead agent, and a dead lawyer, and a dead accountant, and we negotiated and haggled for what seemed an eternity. As soon as the contract was signed I was hurled back into my body. Just as I prepared to cough, open my eyes, and startle the sobbing bystanders by taking a breath, I overheard some academic type among the gawkers say, "You know, the sphincters automatically relax upon death," which kind of ruined the whole near-death experience for me.

TIPS ON HOW TO SURVIVE YOUR NEAR-DEATH EXPERIENCE

A good near-death experience doesn't just happen—like sex or public speaking, you have to be prepared for it. Finally, here's a book to help you plan for that happy almost-ending. *Embarrassed by the Light* covers it all: anecdotes of near-death bummer trips, tips for what to bring along on your journey, advice about thorny legal issues, and guidelines on how to deal with post-death syndrome. Filled with quizzes, case studies, glossaries, and maps, it's the ultimate guide to the penultimate experience.

In this book, I will answer these important questions:

- *What happens if I die on a bad-hair day?*
- *How can I tell if I'm dead or just really drunk?*
- *Will my cellular phone work in the afterworld? Which long-distance carrier is best?*
- *How can I make sure my ex-spouse won't meet me on the other side?*
- *What if I find myself in a tunnel of light, but it's the Lincoln Tunnel?*

From **LIVING END,**
A Catalog for the Near-Death (ND) Aficionado

- **Hemlock Lite** The perfect aperitif for a relaxing near-death adventure.

- **ND-Alert Bracelet** ''In case of sudden death, please don't bother me for a few seconds,'' says this colorful bracelet. Wear it and let friends and strangers give you a chance to enjoy yourself in the other world.

- **Relaxed-Fit Noose** When you want to hang around on the other side but not go all the way, reach for this comfy contraption.

- **Frommer's The Other Side on $5 a Day** Handy ectoplasm format makes this the only guidebook you'll ever need.

- **ND Light Helmet** Don't be blinded by the light—get accustomed to being bathed in that otherworldly glow. S/M/L. Optional halo attachment.

- **SIMDead** Virtual Reality Death Game. Anticipate every twist and turn of the afterlife with this exciting computer simulation. Comes with its own Ouija mouse and Dr. Kevorkian help screens.

- **Chiron Toll Tokens** Why be caught short when it comes time to commute to the other side? Order these handy tokens for that all-so-special journey. Simply slip onto your eyelids before going to sleep each night.

Breathing Exercises: Getting in Shape for the Journey

- **Exercise No. 1**
  Inhale deeply and hold your breath. Keep holding it. Keep holding it. Keeeeeeeep holding it . . .

- **Exercise No. 2**
  Exhale slowly. Hold it. Hold it. Hoooooooold it . . .

- **Exercise No. 3**
  (Note: you will need some duct tape for this one.)
  Take a deep breath. Tape shut your mouth and nostrils. Relax.

Ask Angel

Dear Angel,

If I really died and then came back to life, would I still have to be married to the same person?

—Dying to Know

Dear Dying,

It depends on your vows, but most specify "Till death do us part," which means that a near-death experience can be legally more effective and a lot less expensive than that trip to Reno. But if you exercise the "I was dead and now I'm single and alimony-free" option, you'll have to figure out how to handle your credit cards afterwards.

Dear Angel,

I'm really embarrassed—for years I've been faking all my near-death experiences. Should I tell my husband, or just go on describing how good my other-world journeys were?

—Grave Doubts

Dear Grave,

It's too late now to come clean—the past is dead. Concentrate on the present, and work harder to have that peak experience. (Consult the exercises in this book—there are simple ways you and your husband can work together to achieve better, and even simultaneous, quasi-mortems.)

Dear Angel,
While watching PBS the other night, I could swear I had a near-death experience. Is this possible?

—Pledge Knight

Dear Pledge,
Many people have reported crossing to the otherworld during PBS nature specials and even BBC historical dramas. Other triggers for near-death trips include certain government jobs, the Academy Awards ceremony, and the lines at Disney World.

The Farm

Farmer Brown studied Michael's résumé for the hundredth time. He shifted the toothpick from the left side of his mouth to the right, and tipped the straw hat back on his head. "Yep, sonny, you'll do."

Michael was first in his class at Harvard Medical School. He planned to become a plastic surgeon in Southern California, earning $3 million a year while increasing the sum total of beauty in the world and soaking up some rays.

Then Michael got a call from the Central Iowa Feed and Seed Cooperative. They wanted to interview him for a job.

"You want me to be a sodbuster?" Michael said incredulously. "Are you *nuts*?"

Farmer Brown reminded Michael that agriculture had saved more lives than all the medical advances of history combined. Chastened, Michael agreed to stop by for an interview.

"It's two thousand dollars an hour, with six thousand an hour for overtime. You're paid for twelve-hour days, though we only expect you to work two and then sleep the rest of the time behind the barn. You get a bonus for all that you grow. You get a bigger bonus for everything you don't grow, thanks to the farm subsidy program. You have six months of paid vacation each year, and can retire in five years at double salary."

Michael was dubious. "What about benefits?"

"You get a custom-made, chauffeur-driven Lamborghini tractor. Monogrammed Brolio overalls and Gucci work boots. Health care is thrown in, complete with rabies and tetanus shots."

"Hmmmmm, I don't know. I kind of had my heart set on medicine."

"Ah, there's no future in medicine. Farming is the way to go. Did I mention that we buy your house, clothes, food, and everything else? We also guarantee that you win at least three blue ribbons per year at the county fair."

"What's the catch?"

"Catch?" Brown asked. "Why should there be a catch? This is America. It's a wonderful country. Oh, we pay for your funeral, too, if you happen to have an accident on the job, if you know what I mean."

Babs, Michael's wife, was delighted. "Let's go for it."

Avery Tex, the hired hand to whom Michael was assigned during his first few weeks, was a morose but hard-working individual.

"Avery," Michael asked one day as they cleaned out the pigsties, "How come sixteen hands on this farm died last year?" Commemorative brass plaques adorned the horse stalls in the barn.

Avery fixed Michael with a baleful stare. "It's called attrition, Michael. Happens in any profession. And some of those hands stuck their fingers where they didn't belong, like in the farm implements."

Twice a week Michael and Avery loaded up the wagon and took produce into town to sell at the Organic Food Mart. They returned with a cargo of mysterious barrels.

"What's in the mysterious barrels, Avery?" Michael asked.

"None of your business, Michael," Avery replied.

A hidden microphone in the wagon chassis transmitted their conversation to a high-tech control room in the top of the Brown farm silo, where the sinister Thrasher Hogwash bent over a receiver. "I don't trust this new guy," Hogwash muttered to himself. "He asks too many questions."

Michael grew strong and bronzed tilling the soil. The feel of the earth and smell of manure made him forget medicine altogether. He was happy, and decided to be the best hand Farmer Brown had ever seen. Babs had a secret fling with a *National Geographic* photographer. She was happy, too.

One day a stranger accosted Michael. "I'm Agent Clarence of the U.S. Department of Agriculture. Did you know that the Brown farm secretly uses pesticides and chemical fertilizer, and then sells its crops as organic produce? They also launder stolen frozen food, which they sell at roadside stands as garden fresh."

"I don't believe it," Michael said, spitting a stream of tobacco juice.

"It's true. Workers in sweatshops concealed under the fields thaw out frozen peas, make little green pods out of papier-mâché, and then glue them together."

"Can you make money at that?" Michael asked.

"Well, their prices are pretty steep," Clarence replied.

"How do they get away with it?"

"They are fiendishly cautious. Those sixteen other hands suspected something and were murdered by the sales rep for the chemical company. We want you to help us blow the lid off the operation."

"What harm does it do?"

"Probably none. But it's *nasty* to lie to people. Think of all those poor duped vegans."

The next day Hogwash confronted Michael in the outhouse. "Don't talk to Clarence again. I have pictures of you looking kind of funny at the sheep. You wouldn't want your wife or child to see them, now would you?"

"I don't have a child," Michael replied.

"We adopted one for you and are raising him in a fancy prep school back east. We've taught him to think the world of you, Michael. You wouldn't want to betray the poor lad's love and trust?" Hogwash grinned wickedly.

A chill ran down Michael's spine. My God, these people covered everything, would stop at nothing!

Michael pondered his plight for a long time. If he blew the whistle, the farmers would turn him into fertilizer. If he didn't, the USDA would get him. He wasn't sure what the USDA could do, but he'd seen their blue-inked stamp on the carcasses of dead animals, a memory that filled him with dread.

"Okay, Clarence," Michael said the next day. They met in the west pasture, disguised as cows. "For $5 million and enrollment in the USDA witness protection program, we're in."

Over the following weeks, Michael worked like a man possessed. He hired an inventor and commissioned him to develop a photocopy machine with an automatic feed that would take barrels. With it he could slip into the locked third subbasement of the barn, copy all of the labels in less than a minute, and then sneak out again before anyone noticed. He took clippings from plants all over the farm and sent them to three independent chemical assay labs around the country. The next time Avery took the wagon into town, Michael surreptitiously followed him. He drove the combine, fearful that Avery might recognize the tractor.

Eventually Michael collected all the information he could possibly need: ten thousand photocopies of labels, scraps of papier-mâché, samples of green paint, frozen food wrappers—all meticulously organized and labeled. It wouldn't be enough for convictions but, armed with this information, the USDA could get search warrants.

Hogwash began to grow suspicious when he saw Michael driving the copy machine on a forklift truck around the barnyard. So he bugged every ear of corn on the farm, hid miniature video cameras in the potatoes, and recorded every single thing that went on. Unfortunately for him, this was too much information to handle, so the diabolical surveillance program was an utter waste of time.

Michael noticed the hidden microphones and cameras and grew more fretful. He also noticed the extra cows who appeared in greater numbers every day. He deduced from the way they ran when a bull entered the pasture that they must be USDA men in disguise. Hunted and hounded on every side, unable to trust anyone, he loaded his bales of documents in a hay wagon, hitched it to the Lamborghini tractor, and with Babs at his side, set off for Miami. Why Miami? Who knows?

The two sides began closing in. Farmer Brown and Hogwash dispatched armies of armed farmers, while the USDA marshaled every packing house and shrimp boat inspector at its disposal. Miami became a city under siege, with everyone looking for Michael.

The locals were befuddled by the sudden influx of off-season tourists—a multitude of pitchfork-toting farmers in overalls and a comparable number of weird men in hip boots and aprons covered in blood or fish scales.

"Gosh, Effie," one Miami giftshop owner commented to his wife. "First it was the old folks and college kids from up north, then the Cubans from down south. And now it's this—whatever *this* is!"

It was a tense time, replete with all the usual narrow escapes, clever moves on the part of our hero, blunders by the bad guys, surprise betrayals, quick plot twists and turns, more narrow misses, tons of success, shots fired, a dead guy. In the end, of course, Michael and Babs got away, retired to a tropical island with mountains of loot, having left all the evidence behind for Clarence (poor hard-working slob!) so that he could lock up the bad guys and render the world safe for democracy and vegetarians.

The
SEVEN HABITS OF
HIGHLY DEFECTIVE
PEOPLE

Powerful Lessons in Personal Repugnance

STEVEN I. COVET

of the Covet Your Neighbor's Wife Institute for Defectiveness
Salt Lake City, Utah

D id you ever hear about the concept of a *paradigm*? I first discovered the word *paradigm* when I was forty, and since then I've noticed that I make money whenever I use it. For one thing, people are impressed that I can pronounce it—that silent "g" can be tricky! The word also makes them nervous because it could be one of those figures from geometry they can't remember, or some obscure Greek philosopher. Folks who are anxious and intimidated tend to fork over big bucks for products that feed into their insecurities, like self-help books that promise to significantly change their lives.

So I use *paradigm* on practically every page of this book, even though I don't have the slightest idea what it means. Why do I have a habit of using words I don't understand? Because I am a *highly defective* communicator. Being highly defective has brought me much success in life. It got you to buy this book, and it enables me to fill its pages with endless anecdotes about my life and family without feeling any pressure to make sense at all. I am living proof that *you too can turn your bad habits into HIGHLY DEFECTIVE behavior*. In fact, anyone reading this book has the potential to become America's *MOST DEFECTIVE LEADER*, and that's saying a lot, since the competition is rather fierce.

Here's a diagram that explains my paradigm of how *paradigm*, my own defectiveness, and Simon & Schuster have come together to bring you this book, which will forever alter how you see me, yourself, and AT&T commercials:

PARADIGM

MY DEFECTIVENESS	SIMON & SCHUSTER

By the way, I'll be breaking up the text with a lot of these neat diagrams, so get ready for some very exciting visuals here. And, while we're on the subject of visuals, just let me tell you that you can get more out of my ideas and I can get even more out of you if you sign up for one-on-one sessions with me or one of my highly trained, defective staff members. We have programs and prices to suit everyone in America, no matter what their range of competence. Our special week-long "Defective Habit-a-Day" seminar starts at only $650 per hour, and we at the Covet Your Neighbor's Wife Institute for Defectiveness will hold it anywhere—at your home, in your office, or even aboard our own Covet aircraft carrier in the Persian Gulf. It's your choice, of course, but I'm just warning you: it's more expensive to do sessions, but it's a lot more pleasant than getting all the way through this book. So just call 1–800-SCREWUP and our highly defective salespeople will book you within twenty-four hours.

While I'm waiting for you to call, I might as well begin the book here with one of those APPROPRIATE ANECDOTES/MYTHIC STORIES (AA/MS) that are so inspirational when you're trying to access your personal power and change your paradigm. You'll know when one of these is coming along because I'll throw in one of those **BOLDFACE HEADLINES** that signal AA/MS, like this:

THE SEVEN DWARFS: THE GIANTS OF HABITS

Do you remember the story of Snow White and the Seven Dwarfs? No? That's okay—I don't either, but I have these wonderful college kids who intern here for nothing, and I got one of them to rent the movie and write an action memo about it. Seems that there's this damsel in distress and she ends up in a pigsty with seven highly defective guys. Their very names are symbols of their bad habits. Sneezy didn't take enough vitamin C, and Grumpy failed at his course in learned optimism. Dopey was a kind of pre–Forrest Gump guy who couldn't tap into his stupidity, while Doc was one of those right-wing intellectuals who kept bemoaning the closing of the American mind. Sleepy was a narcoleptic, Bashful had attention deficit disorder, and Happy was addicted to tranquilizers.

Now, what does their story have to offer us? Simply this: Although personally repugnant and defective, *the seven dwarfs were interpersonal giants!* They got exactly what they wanted all the time because they used their disgusting personalities and weaknesses to manipulate Snow White and become policymakers in the Prince's country. Because they were incompetent, Snow White cleaned their house, cooked their meals, provided them with some innocent sexual daydreams, and opened them up to the idea of pets. By faking her own death with a poisoned apple, she let the dwarfs believe they were seeing a miracle when she came back, and she helped them live happily ever after as loyal hangers-on rather than gritty mine workers. The seven dwarfs were naturals—they were, without even trying much, *HIGHLY DEFECTIVE PEOPLE!*

If you look at the following diagram, you can see the Seven Dwarf Paradigm as it applies to our main subject at hand:

Bashful, Sleepy, Sneezy, Grumpy, Dopey, Doc, Happy

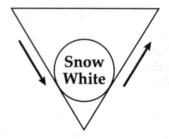

Aren't these diagrams great? I'll let you in on a little secret: My kids do them! Every week we hold a family meeting and after I yell at them a while and miscommunicate and generally terrorize them, at least one of the nine little whippersnappers will volunteer to draw something so they can get a tiny bit of extra candy that week.

Well, enough of this heavy mythical stuff. It's no wonder such a highly defective leader as Walt Disney was attracted to this Snow White stuff—it's a powerful paradigm, especially for guys who plan to freeze themselves for centuries.

Now let's get to the meat of my program. In this book, you can work your way through all seven habits to become a highly defective person. I strongly recommend that after you finish developing the first three habits, you take some time to practice before going on to even more defective strategies. Why? Probably because I wanted to put some cool stuff and diagrams between Habit 3 and Habit 4. Why are there seven habits? Damned if I know. Mostly because I couldn't think of any more. Besides, seven is a real mystical number, and if seven was a good enough number for God, it should be good enough for me, at least until I get my own cable network.

HABIT 1

BE PROPHYLACTIC

People ask me, "Are you sure you don't mean *proactive*?" No, I don't! Being proactive is assertive and positive. We are talking about defective thinking here, and what better way to think about *that* than with a prophylactic? To be truly defective, you must insulate yourself from others in a kind of latex haze that will diminish your pleasure and the pleasure of those around you. You should sheath yourself in smugness and despair before entering a touchy situation. In short, think of yourself as a human condom in search of . . . well . . . not much.

The difference between a proactive person who takes charge and a prophylactic person whose anxieties just grow and grow as he or she sits around protected from the dangers of the world is just like night and day. I think. Except that this isn't making any sense. So let me tell you a little story.

A friend of mine lived with a roommate who was a real go-getter. First in his class at Harvard Business School, windsurfer, semipro baseball player and golfer. This guy never even used a car—he ran from place to place in whatever weather. One day it was raining hard, and my friend's roommate dashed out to jog to his office eight miles away. Before he left he made fun of my friend, who was thinking of not going to his job as assistant manager at the local McDonald's because he didn't have a raincoat and he might get wet on the way to his Yugo.

Well, my friend stayed home and someone called from a radio station offering him a cash jackpot of $95,000 and when he was on his way the next (sunny) day to the station to pick up his check, he got hit by a truck and received a settlement for $3.5 million. His roommate was downsized from his job shortly thereafter, joined the Peace Corps, and was eaten by a tribe of gentrified cannibals who prefer low-fat runners.

Now, why was my friend so defective and so successful? *Because he lived his life prophylactically—no raincoat, no action!*

Application Suggestions:
1. Either go out and buy a raincoat or throw your raincoat away.
2. Listen to the radio a lot.
3. Identify opportunities where it helps to think prophylactically—for example, do you know anything about how the condom market is influencing the stocks of pharmaceutical companies?

HABIT 2
BEGIN AND NEVER FINISH

I'd like to explain what this means, but I believe in showing instead of telling. I began this section without any intention of ever following through. I simply lost interest in this particular habit, but that doesn't mean that it's not one of the most defective habits. In fact, I recommend it for anyone striving to become highly defective. You only need one action chart to practice and perfect this habit. Basically, you make a list of what you want to do, and then you put a line after it and a dot that represents your life (see diagram below). If you ever fill in the chart before you die, you have become too effective.

Point A   Point B

Task: _____•Death

Application Suggestions:
1. Always read the last chapter of a book first.
2.
3.

HABIT 3
PICK YOUR NOSE

S ometimes I wonder how this one got in here, but we had to stretch the material, and I thought if I put it pretty much in the middle, maybe nobody would notice. I do, however, recommend this behavior as a power strategy. I often pick my nose on trains and airplanes to keep other people from talking to me and interrupting my time for meditating on my defectiveness. Here's how it works:

Picking Nose
in Middle Seat
of a Plane

DIAGRAM A

Picking Nose in
Aisle Seat
of a Plane

DIAGRAM B

Picking Nose in
Window Seat
of a Plane

DIAGRAM C

Personally, I recommend the Diagram A approach as most efficiently defective. You can gross out two people at the same time.

Application Suggestions:
1. Don't be afraid to be picky.
2. Think green and clean.
3. Let your fingers do the walking.

INTERLUDE: PARADIGMS OF INTERDEFECTIVENESS

Now that you've mastered the first three habits, you're probably ready to hear some more of my endless anecdotes and nutty theories about how people become successful defectives. This is the part of the book where I introduce more philosophical underpinnings and definitions. Like the *emotional bank account*. An effective person has an *emotional bank account* at one of those new interstate banks that are giving away twenty-five-inch color TV sets. A highly defective person's *emotional bank account* is centered around one of those twenty-four-hour check-cashing services where you're about to pass a rubber check.

Now here's another heavy thought: *you cannot be truly defective alone.* If a tree is defective alone in the forest, does anyone notice? No, you must be *interdefective* with other people. You must analyze how other people's defects feed into yours, and how you can manipulate the situation to become even more defective. Say, for example, you are a terrible listener and tend to ignore the needs of those around you. Maybe your boss is a screaming nincompoop who never thinks before talking and is constantly assaulting you with his verbal tirades. But do you care? No—because you have developed your defect, which just happens to mesh perfectly with his. *You have become interdefective, and thus ready to fail in tandem.*

To understand this concept further, please consult the diagram on right. (However, just in case it makes no sense, you should know that my wife took the kids away for vacation and for once I hired an artist who turned out to be stupid and partially blind, and I've never been good at all at explaining *anything*.)

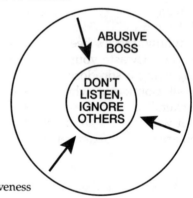

The Circle of Interdefectiveness

Okay, back to those pesky habits . . .

Habit 4

Think: Loser Wins

Did you ever hear that rhyme, "Finders keepers/Losers weepers?" Yeah, I did, too. So what? You must really think I'm a loser if you think I can make that little poem last for a few pages.

Anyhow, there's been a lot of talk about win/win vs. win/lose attitudes. Don't waste your time. You want to be defective, and that means losing. Being a sore loser is even more defective. I recommend that you tape all politicians who make bitter concession speeches (the Nixon "Checkers" one is my favorite) and play them over and over. Practice whining—it will get you what you want. Remember, we live in an age of guilt. If you are seen as oppressed in any way, you will gain strength. *Loser wins!*

Habit 5

Don't Try to Understand Anything

Things change all the time. So why bother getting a handle on them? Lots of people waste time daily trying to make sense of the world. You could better use this time watching TV, playing computer games, or even picking your nose.

I had a friend who was a seeker. He traveled the world looking for knowledge. He studied with gurus and acupuncturists and shamans. Then he returned home and started a successful high-tech company. He was legendary in the business—he held weekly meetings with all his employees. He listened to their concerns. He offered them excellent benefits. He really tried to understand them.

In time, the employees unionized and filed many suits against my friend. He lapsed into depression and eventually choked to death on some brown rice while listening to a Ravi Shankar album. He had tried to be an effective listener. He had tried to understand. *To be highly defective, you cannot understand anything!*

Habit 6
Don't Write Thank-You Notes

T his is a real pet peeve with me. What is America coming to, anyway? I speak all over the country and so my mailbox and e-mail are just stuffed with lugs *thanking* me for coming. Don't they know I get paid for it? Don't they have other stuff to do? Writing thank-you notes or even just saying "thank you" is a habit people often begin quite early in life. I prefer the defective approach, as shown in the flowchart below:

Effective**
Good deed/gift ———> Sap ———> Thank-you note

Defective**
Good deed/gift —> Self-centered defective type —> Resounding silence

Pop Quiz:
How many times have I mentioned my wife's name in this book? My children's?
Am I bald, or do I have hair?

HABIT 7
GET BURNED OUT AND USE OLD SAWS

S ometimes, I have to say that my plan for success is amazingly simple: Squander your emotional, psychological, and physical resources, develop unhealthy habits that lead to defectiveness, and then just watch what happens. A lot of other motivational speakers will tell you to go back to the well, renew yourself, sharpen the old saw. I say: Why? When you're burned out, other people have to take care of you. You've finally gone through emotional bankruptcy and now you're on mental Medicaid.

Let me quote from Quentin Crisp here: "You fall out of your mother's womb, you crawl across open country under fire, and drop into your grave." Or, if you prefer, Thoreau: "What men call good fellowship is commonly but the virtue of pigs in a litter which lie close together to keep each other warm." Or how about Huey Long: "Hard work is damn near as overrated as monogamy."

How We Fly

SHERMAN NEWLIN, M.D.

AUTHOR'S NOTE

I was going to thank my agent and editor and secretary and friends for suggesting this topic and title and helping me through the process of writing this book but, quite frankly, it has been a nightmare from start to finish. It was all a misunderstanding. I'm getting old and my hearing is no longer what it was, and I honestly believed my agent wanted me to write a book called **How We Fly**. And then when the contract was drawn up and signed, and the sales force was plugging it for all they were worth and the advance orders came raining in, it was too late to change.

REVIVING OEDIPUS

■

DOMESTICATING THE SEXUALITY OF YOUR ADOLESCENT BOY

SOPHOCLES SMITH, PH.D.
CASSANDRA MEDEA

Everybody who has survived adolescence knows how confusing and stressful it can be. For young boys, the teenage years often become a perilous time when they go out of control, experimenting with unsafe sex, drugs, and fast cars. As parents, we can help our sons through these troubled times by accessing the myth of Oedipus, the Greek king who found happiness and then tragedy in the arms of his mother, Jocasta.

Freud recognized the Oedipus complex as a normal developmental stage. Boys naturally want to sleep with their mothers. And yet so few young men get the opportunity. Why? Why, we want to know, are young men being left without direction to wander the streets and malls of America when they could be safe at home with Mom, learning to unleash their repressed potential for sexual happiness? Parents looking for a way to keep young boys busy and out of trouble need look no further than their own bedroom door.

This is a new world far different than the one we grew up in, and it calls for new psychological strategies for helping our sons become strong, secure men. In *Reviving Oedipus*, we discuss how families can overcome outdated taboos to create an exciting learning environment for their adolescent sons.

Sections include:

- *The Jocasta Factor:* Why Mom is a safe, experienced sex partner who can be trusted.
- *The Intimate Rival:* How Dad can cope easily with the competition, knowing that he controls his rival's allowance and that he will leave home in just a few years.
- *Sphinx Talk:* Helping your son unravel the riddle of sex and love.

Protective Eyegear Included With Every Book!

Nine Stupid Things Women Do to Mess Up Their Clothes

LAURA SAMSONITE

Finally, an Out-of-the-Closet guide to controlling
your relationship with all the dresses, suits,
sweaters, and assorted outfits in your life.

Women and clothes—it's a love–hate relationship. You're attracted to
clothes, you bring them home, you wear them for a while, and then, little
by little, they let you down. They look good on the hanger but they mock
you when you're out together in public. They become more difficult to
maintain or they expose your figure flaws. Finally, they break your heart

and you're out shopping for new ones, trying to forget how worn out and passionless your last duds seemed when you parted company.

Your sartorial relationships don't always have to end in tatters. Now you can break the cycle of wardrobe despair and discouragement by recognizing the nine stupid off-the-rack mistakes that can ruin your clothes and your life. In *Nine Stupid Things Women Do to Mess Up Their Clothes*, you will learn how to control the clothes *and* the skeletons hanging in your closet. (And our special Action Tips will help you develop a step-by-step strategy to eliminate all clothing hassles!)

9 Stupid Things Women Do to Mess Up Their Clothes

No. 1   WOMEN EAT

It's a well-known fact that eating can wreak havoc with your wardrobe, and yet millions of women around the world continue to indulge in this damaging and self-defeating practice. Why? They simply can't stop themselves.

Consider Myra, 39. She has been eating all her life, and this nonstop nutritional search has definitely taken its toll on her closet. "I spill things," she admits, "and the stuff comes back from the dry cleaner with those little pathetic notes saying they were unable to completely remove the stains. I have several white blouses that I can only wear under sweaters, and lots more cuffs of jackets that have been dipped in mustard and spaghetti sauce."

Sue, 46, tells an even sadder story about the effects of appetite on her relationship with clothing. "I have every size from 4 up to 16 hanging in my closet. When I eat too much, my clothing bunches up around my stomach and arms. Then I diet and for a while I fit into smaller sizes, but I always end up at the big-size end of my rack."

Women, how can you avoid these stupid things? Action tips:

- **If you eat, do it in the nude. Not only will this prevent stains on clothing, but it will restrict your eating pattern to certain times. (For example, it will be harder to eat at the office.)**
- **Don't eat. Really. Enough said.**

No. 2 WOMEN COOK

Like eating, its sister dysfunctional behavior, cooking, can be disastrous for fine garments. Our mothers coped with it by wearing dorky aprons, but we know better. If women are to remain truly safe from messing up their clothes, they must avoid cooking altogether. "I tried actually cooking dinner once," says Karen, 27, "and my husband had the nerve to say that my sweater smelled like onions." Don't let it happen to you.

If you can't stand the heat, get out of the kitchen. Action tips:

- **Eat raw foods only!**
- **If you must cook, nuke!!! The microwave is the least messy gadget in your kitchen.**

No. 3   WOMEN DRIVE

"I still remember those black pumps," says Clarissa, 52, wiping away the tears. "They were my favorite shoes until the clutch ruined them forever." Tammy, 29, was having a wonderful day until she realized that a part of her brand new raincoat had been dragging outside her car door for over twenty miles. "I wondered why people were honking at me," says Tammy, who was interviewed at the new part-time job she has taken to pay for another coat.

It's time to shift gears, and consider how dangerous clothed driving can be. Action tips:

- **Drive automatic if you want to save shoes!**
- **Wear short coats and try, when at all possible, to sit on the passenger side!**
- **If buying a new car, inquire about the effects of that model's airbags and safety restraints on different fabrics, such as silk, rayon, and fine wool.**

No. 4   WOMEN PUMP GAS

Petroleum spills might be killing off endangered birds, but their effects are probably even more noticeable on your chenille sweater. There's only one Action tip:

- **Move to a state that makes it illegal to pump your own gas, such as New Jersey!**

No. 5   WOMEN GET MARRIED

Many men are clothing impaired—living in close quarters with them can increase the death toll in your wardrobe.

"Tim thought he was being a great guy when he volunteered to do the laundry," remembers Lois, 26. "He was real surprised when he took my cashmere sweater out of the dryer and it fit our miniature poodle. I cried for a week."

Men can be hazardous to fine garments. Action tip:

- **Keep separate closets!**

No. 6   WOMEN HAVE CHILDREN

Spit, vomit, Play-Doh, fingerpaint, dirt, Magic Marker, glue, grease, popsicles, grape juice, etc. Kids and clothes just don't mix. "Joshua has destroyed at least $500 worth of my clothing," says Jennifer, a first-time mother at 33. Action tips:

- **Practice birth control!**
- **Shrink-wrap children daily in protective Saran Wrap!**

No. 7   WOMEN WORK

Running to the office, running *in* the office—the terrible price of shredding pantyhose keeps the American economy going. Not to mention the hazards of coffee and ink stains and those little screws on chairs that rip at hems.

Action tips:

- **Work in a disposable paper jumpsuit!**
- **Get a job at a nudist colony!**

No. 8   WOMEN SLEEP WITH RIPPERS

It is a male fantasy to rip clothing from women's bodies. Usually, men who do this have seen too many sex scenes in Michael Douglas movies. If you are or have been involved with a ripper, you know what a turnoff it can be as he excitedly pops the buttons from your $175 blouse. "I always tell guys: Rip my silk negligee, and you're dead meat," explains Beverly, 69, who has avoided messing up her clothes for decades.

Action tips:

- **Always undress before bed, even sometimes during dinner!**
- **Make him buy all your clothes, or at least sew them up again afterwards!**

No. 9   WOMEN MENSTRUATE

It's hell on the underwear, girls. Action tips:

- **Wear those wing-things all the time!**
- **Pray for early menopause!**

A YEAR IN POMPEII

PETER MAGMA

THE YEAR WAS SHORT and hot.

My wife and I had come here often before as tourists, dousing our senses for a few delicious, short weeks at a time in the sun, the greens, the blues, the scents that wafted in from unknown lands, the touch, the sounds—all of which consumed us with magnificent, lasting impressions that would see us through the long, cold winter months. But at last we had decided to live here forever, transforming transient glories into eternal bliss.

It was late August A.D. 79 when we arrived and began fixing up the old farmhouse on the road to Herculaneum. Pliny the Elder, a friend of many years, brought bread, wine, and salt as a welcome gift. Pliny the Younger—''Junior,'' as everyone called him—had recently left home, and ''Pops'' felt the need for company.

Soon the dust and cinders spewed from Mount Vesuvius, covering everything twenty feet deep, while the sulfurous smoke choked everyone to death.

"This is a charming local custom," my wife said. "Is this how all newcomers are welcomed?"

"Ah! Oooooh! Eeeek! Yikes!" Pliny replied, before lapsing into a taciturn silence.

Our neighbors had been charming people who grew and cooked splendid traditional food. They would chat of this and that during the long Mediterranean evenings, telling tales of other times. Alas, they were buried alive before we'd had the pleasure of meeting them.

My wife and I realized that we had made a poor choice of homes, or at least had picked the wrong year.

THE BELLBOTTOM CURVE

RICHARD J. ARMANI
CHARLES MIZRAHI

Many will find this study disturbing. This book is about the complex relationship between intellectual capacity and clothes. Contemporary Americans are inclined to believe that clothes are simply a fashion statement, or perhaps an unacknowledged function of habit or peer pressure. Supposedly enlightened thinkers shy from the ancient credo that "the clothes make the man." Our research, however, proves the truth of this saying, whose only flaw is its limited scope. Clothes *do* make the man, and also the woman, and the child, and, for those who dress up their dogs or put straw hats on cart horses, the beast.

"Yes, yes," our colleagues all say, "but smart people are also often those who know how to function well within society. This includes dressing and behaving in socially acceptable ways."

"What about Howard Hughes?" we ask. "What about Bill Gates, or the artist formerly known as Prince?"

"Wait," they reply testily. "Do you really mean to say you believe that what you wear determines what you are?"

Yes, we do. And we have thirty years of data to prove it.

Chapter 1
Cognitive Class and Attire,
1965–1995

Extensive surveys among bellbottom-wearing young persons residing in major metropolitan areas during the years 1965–1969 reveal that they tended to be politically liberal and generally open-minded and free-thinking in their attitudes toward life.

In a major follow-up study, these same young people, by now somewhat older, were surveyed again between 1993 and 1995 and evaluated for clothing style, political beliefs, and general social philosophy.

Surprisingly, our results tended to strongly support our personal preconceptions and the intended conclusions of our study. As the proportion of people wearing bellbottom trousers declined, political conservatism and rigidity of views on social policy in general increased proportionately. The intelligence of the study population also dramatically increased, as measured in terms of their agreement with our personal views about what is important in life and what one really needs to know in order to succeed.

Bellbottom frequency is merely one sartorial measure of intelligence, but serves in a particularly striking way to illustrate the fundamental principles of our study. Other measures are discussed in the appendices.

Chapter 2
The Demography of Intelligence

In addition to the cohort study discussed in the previous chapter, where we followed a single population over time, we carried out a random cross-sectional study of society as a whole.

Randomly surveying customers who made purchases at ten of the finer Fifth Avenue clothing stores in New York, we found that they tended to be well-adjusted, thriving members of society. No ill-clad or marginal people were detected in the test population.

As a measure of intelligence we asked whether they agreed with the statement: "The clothes someone is wearing is one of the most important indicators of his/her true worth." The customers almost universally agreed with this statement, demonstrating their deft grasp of one of the most useful truths in modern life.

As a uniform control population we studied various groups of uniformed employees, including hotel maids, sanitation workers, and convicted felons. They generally tended to be poorly dressed, and often disagreed with the statement: "The clothes someone is wearing is one of the most important indicators of his/her true worth." This demonstrated their failure to comprehend a vital fact about the world in which they live, which may account for the relatively low-status occupations in which most of them were employed.

Chapter 3
Location, Attire, and Intelligence

"How can clothes possibly determine someone's personality?" our colleagues ask us, ever more shrilly as time goes on. Without a theoretical construct or causal mechanism to account for a phenomenon, even solid evidence always remains slightly suspect, tinged by the possibility of statistical error.

The explanation is very simple. So simple that, in retrospect, it is very difficult to imagine how previous investigators have not hit upon it.

People who live in France are French. Those who reside in China are Chinese. Finns, according to an elegantly simple equation, are people from Finland. This formula, which we call the "Locus Identifier," applies to all parts of the globe and thus comes as close as a social science generalization can to being a universal principle.

Nation $\lozenge$ (people who live there) $\subseteq$ Nationality

THE LOCUS IDENTIFIER

Nationality, of course, is a fundamental determiner of who and what a person is, as any bigot knows. Think of virtually any nationality and you can attach to it a set of widely accepted characteristics, including level of intelligence. Intelligence, then, is largely determined by nationality.

A nation or country is simply a place. It is where one is, or the place that

A nation or country is simply a place. It is where one is, or the place that one's in. What are clothes but smaller places, smaller things that one is in? And if the big place one is in determines intelligence, it clearly follows that a smaller place—one that hugs one's being more closely, more intimately, with greater accuracy—should determine intelligence more closely.

Chapter 4
The Clothes Make the Country

When one thinks carefully about the concepts described in the last chapter, another exciting possibility begins to emerge. Nationality, we said, determines intelligence. But is it nationality, or is it national costume? Consider the designer clothes of the Soviet Union and other Eastern Bloc nations. Think of the clothes in Communist China. Now think of the designer clothes from France and Italy, or even of England's Savile Row. Need one look farther for an explanation of the differing political, economic, and social conditions that prevail in the nations of the world?

Chapter 5
How to Make Things Better

The problem with social policy in the United States, as in many other developed nations, is that governments try to solve social problems without attacking their root cause. Why pour billions of dollars into education and other such programs when we could take the much more direct approach of providing subsidized nice designer clothes for everyone? A person who looks better feels better, and *is* better. A dapper nation is a happy nation.

IRON TOM

*Helping Your Neutered Cat
Regain His Masculinity*

ROBERTSON BLY

The Iron Tom Myth

Once upon a time, in a kingdom high upon a hill above a forest, there lived a poor bedraggled alley cat who had given birth to ten kittens. It was a snowy winter, and this alley cat was young and inexperienced, but she knew that her kittens would not live long unless she could find them a dry, warm place. So one windy day she left them along the corner of the town wall, covering their little furless bodies as best she could with some oak leaves, and set off to find a better home for her litter.

Almost as soon as the she-cat left, a soaring hawk, spying the wriggling creatures under the leaves, swooped down to investigate. "Ten tasty snacks!" said he, and proceeded to devour the tiny kits one by one. All but the last one—the hawk was getting full, and he noticed that the last one wasn't moving anymore. "I'm not eating something dead when I've had my fill of tasty, squirmy tidbits," he said, and took off, leaving the last kitten all alone on the cold pavement.

Upon her return, the mother cat cried out in anguish. Only one little cat left! And he was turning blue. Even as she sat patiently licking him, she feared he would never return to life, and she cursed herself for ever leaving her kittens alone.

But the mother's warm sandpapery tongue worked miracles, and the kitten did not pass on to its next life. Instead, he lived and prospered, growing furry and roly-poly in the little straw nest his mother built for him in the castle's dairy stable, the home she had found on the fateful day when all his brothers and sisters had been eaten by the hawk.

One day the king's daughter, a beautiful golden-haired princess, came to watch the cows get milked. It was very early in the morning, and she was not used to getting up early, so she sat down on a haystack and began to drift off to sleep. The little kitten had been taught by his mother *never* to go near human beings, but his mother *was* out hunting mice, and he *was* hungry, so he got up to see if he could lap up some of the spilt milk that was sometimes around the stable. When he left his cozy nest, he spied the dozing princess. She was the most wondrous creature he had ever seen. Her dress shimmered with golden brocade, and dangling across her breasts were strings of tiny beads that moved ever so slightly when she breathed. Her golden locks bobbed up and down in the gentle breeze. In spite of all the warnings his mother had given him, the little cat began creeping closer and closer to the sleeping beauty, and before long he sat on her shoulder purring, playing with her golden curls.

The princess awoke with a start and screamed, causing the little cat to jump on her head and scratch her forehead. When the princess recovered her wits and saw the little cat cowering under a manure shovel, his fur puffing him up to twice his size, she softened and began to laugh. "Come here, you fuzzy little fellow," she said in a high-pitched voice, and when the little cat looked into her eyes he could see only love. But he was still too frightened to approach her.

The princess began visiting the dairy stable every day, leaving tidbits of fish and meat for the little cat and his mother. Still, the mother-cat did not trust humans, and she forbade her kitten to go near the girl. But one day when the mother cat was out hunting, the little cat became brave enough to go up to the princess and rub against her leg. She began petting him in ways that reminded him of the soft touch of his mother's tongue, and he heard himself purring.

The princess picked him up and said, "Come live with me at the castle. We have lots of mice, and I would feed you scraps from the table. You could sit in front of the fire and always be warm." The little cat thought it seemed a good idea, and as they walked together toward the palace, they could see a crowd gathered on the street. Some horrible ruffians were torturing the little kitten's mother, pelting her with stones! The brave princess ran up and told everyone to stop at once or face her father's dungeon, but she was too late to save the poor mama cat. Her son cuddled with her as her heart slowed, and with her last breath she said, "Oh son, my only son, remember that you are the son of Iron Tom. Be as much a man as he, and remember your poor mother's love."

The kitten was very sad, and it took the princess a long while to convince him to come to the palace. But once there, he began to forget his grief. He climbed the tapestries on the walls and jumped up on the counters of the kitchen to lick the butter. Once the cook caught him dragging a pheasant out the door, and the king would have made the little cat leave had his daughter not started crying. Soon even the king was won over, and tolerated the little cat jumping right into his favorite chair in front of the fire every time he got up to use the royal latrine.

One night, as the nearly full-grown cat nestled against the sleeping princess's shoulder, shedding his black, sooty fur onto her very expensive eiderdown comforter, he heard another cat yowling outside in the moonlight. Stealthily, so as not to wake his mistress, he jumped off the bed and went to the window. Outside, on the castle's ramparts, was a mangy-looking yet magnificent one-eyed male cat. He had long, rusty hair, ears that had been chewed down in fights, half a tail, and a big, oozy sore on his back.

"I, too, would like to caterwaul like you, master cat," called out the young cat humbly. "Who are you?"

"I am Iron Tom," wailed the old he-cat.

"Father! You have come for me!" said his son. "Where do you live?"

"In the forest, on the beaches, on the prairies," said the elder feline.

"But where is your litter box?"

"I have the sands of time, the sands of all the world's beaches," was the cryptic reply.

"And where is your scratching post?"

"The trees of the forest are mine, all the barks that are not the dog's."

The young cat grew very excited. He could scarcely keep himself from leaping from the window sill.

"Oh, Father! Take me with you!" cried the young cat.

Iron Tom looked poignantly into his son's eyes. He could see what a fine young cat warrior he was about to become. He could imagine the pride he would feel when the other cats smelled his newest son's scent. The old cat made a great lion-like roar, and then spoke.

"Are you crazy, son? You've got a great deal here. That fairy princess is treating you damn good. Look at me. I'm a wreck. It's a good thing your mother was young and naive, because it's not easy to attract the broads when your face looks like a rotting potato and your tail is about to fall off. I might only have one eye, but I can see pretty clearly that you lucked out, kid.

"So here's my advice: Stay with this royal dame, stick with the whole deal. Let her do anything to you. Hell, I've heard the stories—they take out your claws, they cut off your balls. But believe me, it's worth it."

With that, Iron Tom leaped off the wall, disappeared into the forest, and never again bothered his son, who would remember for the rest of his long life his father's words of wisdom.

Spray Huts, Kitty Litter Pits, and Dead Beetle Necklaces: Iron Tom Rituals

MAKING PREY BEADS

Help your cat celebrate his prowess as a hunter by crafting ceremonial objects from his kills. He will be very proud that you cared enough to make prey beads, and will feel like a real warrior wearing them on his collar.

Shrunken mouse heads (see instructions below), dead crickets and beetles, and small bird beaks are easy to string and will give a varied texture to the necklace. If you are lucky enough to have a kitty who catches rabbits, remember that bunny ears make wonderful Iron Tom vests that look great with prey beads. (Note: You can keep dead bodies in your freezer until you accumulate enough to make a good-size string of prey beads. By waiting, you'll be able to give your he-cat a great surprise, too!)

Purring in the Belly: Exercises in Masculinity

When you had your cat fixed, you were revealing many negative subconscious beliefs:

- I am afraid of your masculine powers.

- I do not want a cat with nicked ears.

- I do not trust you to use birth control.

- I do not think you would make a good father.

- My furniture and rugs mean more to me than your sex life.

Don't feel badly about any of your past actions. Like the princess in the Iron Tom story, you did what you thought was right to help your cat fit into a softer, more human world.

But think about your cat. He has been cut off from his birthright, his very male identity. No wonder he wakes you up, careens around the house aimlessly, vomits on the rug, or "misses" the litter box.

Happily, it's not too late for your cat to celebrate his maleness. Masculinity is more than just equipment, after all. These exercises are designed to help your cat retrieve his stolen masculinity, and to make you more comfortable with the wildcat lurking inside your feline companion.

LETTING THE TOMCAT OUT OF THE BAG

Get a good, sturdy supermarket bag (the paper kind made out of trees—plastic *will not work*!), open it, and place it on the floor. Grab your cat, put him in the bag, and quickly roll it up. Walk around chanting "Pussycat, pussycat, where have you been?"

Then place the bag back on the floor, open it quickly, and shout, "To the forest, to become Iron Tom!" If your cat feels compelled to scratch you at this moment, accept it as a sign of forgiveness and newfound assertiveness.

STARE-WAY TO HEAVEN

Your cat has telepathic powers, and anything you communicate to him silently, with soulful eye contact, will mean much more to him than words. Pick a quiet time and get down to your cat's eye level. Stare into his orbs and visualize how his life could have been as a swaggering, dirty, yowling Lothario. Communicate these thoughts to him, and then pick one of his more wonderful physical attributes and concentrate on it, making a connection between his lost sexuality and what attractiveness he still has left. When I do this exercise with my cat Monty, I use the silent chant "Big Paws, Big Paws, Big Paws." And I always let Monty outstare me—it makes him feel powerful.

CREATIVE CATERWAULING
Your cat might never have experienced the joy of sexual screaming. It's up to you to let him know that strange guttural noises are natural, and that you did not have his vocal cords neutered along with his nether parts. Go around the house yowling, and encourage him to join you. (Note: Some people feel too self-conscious and can only achieve this caterwauling effect while they themselves are having sex. I do not need to tell you the negative message this is sending to your cat. So, if you want him to feel good about himself, separate sex and screaming in your own life.)

And Bear in Mind . . .
Other Bestsellers

INTERVIEW WITH AN UMPIRE by Anne Brown Rice

The mistress of horror turns her gaze on the game of baseball with this novel about an unworldly ump who goes from stadium to stadium for eternity, living on stale beer and cigarette butts and ballpark frankfurter leavings.

THE CHEESEDOODLE REPORT by Charity Cheesedoodle

Famous trendwatcher Charity Cheesedoodle predicts what the next decade's hottest snack foods will be and how they will coincide with environmental, consumer, and work issues.

WAITING TO EXHALE THROUGH THE HIDDEN SENSES OF LUCK by Sunny Tan Macmillan

A first—a generic novel in which the reader decides on the ethnic background of the characters. Classic mother/daughter, girlfriend/girlfriend, boy/girl stories are enhanced when they reflect your very own heritage—just fill in the blanks for native expressions, food descriptions, and particular cultural neuroses.

"S" IS FOR SUPERCALIFRAGILISTICEXPEALODOCIOUS by Sue Graphite

Detective Kinsey Poppins investigates a murder among the chimney sweeps of London.

THE CAT WHO COUGHED UP A HAIRBALL by Lillian Jackson Browne

Exciting mystery set in a vet's office.

EAT JUNK AND LIVE MINUTES LONGER by Sixpak ChoppedLiver

Do you really need to live for a long time? Face it—if you just had a few extra minutes at the end of your life to get things together, make a few calls—that would be enough, right?

This book shows you two-second daily meditations you can perform while wolfing down a hot dog or swigging back some beer. It's guaranteed to add minutes to your life, or to help you say goodbye swiftly when you feel your corroded arteries giving way.

YOU KNOW YOU GOTTA STOP LAPDANCING WHEN HIS BELLY GETS TOO BIG by Erma LaBomba

America's most beloved femme humorist tackles the zany world of senior sex.

WOMEN WHO RUN WITH THE MALLRATS by Clarissa Benetton

Forget predators: Today's women want to spend time with cute Generation X kids who wear goatees and attend to their every need. This book is filled with inspirational stories about middle-aged women who bought Gap jeans for kids and then experienced the thrill of extreme passion behind the Piercing Pagoda.

MEDITATIONS FOR WOMEN WHO DON'T DO A DAMN THING by Ida LaMoment

Daily inspirational quotations for gals who like to be lazy, such as ''I wonder what's on Oprah today?'' and ''Which chocolate should I have next?''

SMART WOMEN, FOOLISH INVOICES by Lucretia Mint, CPA

For the accountant in every woman, a financial plan that will keep you in the proper billing mood.

PLAY MYST FOR ME by Clint Westwood

Lonely female computer addict stalks a CD-ROM developer in San Francisco.

POLITICALLY CORRECT MEIN KAMPF by Huckleberry Finn Garner

That immortal but oft-neglected classic revised and updated to meet modern needs. Purged of its hatred, ethnocentrism, megalomaniacal aspirations, bigotry, turgid prose, blatant lies, distasteful thoughts, and outright lunacy, this slender pamphlet stands as a touching tale of a nasty Austrian boy and his silly dreams.

JURASSIC PORK by Michael Cretin

Terror strikes at a Central American experimental biogenetic fat farm when great huge women, glutted on fiber and synthetic protein, go on a rampage, devouring fast food, scientists, and lawyers.

AN EVEN BRIEFER HISTORY OF TIME by Stephen W. Hookah

The real problem with time is that there's never enough of it, even to read books about time. Stephen W. Hookah's original ''brief'' best-seller stretched on for page after cryptic page, even though the index shows that time is actually discussed only on pages 8, 15–34, 44, 87, 134, 139, 143–153, and 185. This new abridged edition, issued in handy pamphlet form, eliminates all the other material and delivers just what you want to know.

THE PHYSICIAN'S DESK REFERENCE

The new, updated edition of this indispensable reference work provides a wealth of accumulated medical knowledge. Which desk should you buy? When do you need a desk? How big a desk is appropriate? What sort of adverse design interactions may occur between desks and other articles of office furniture?

THE HORSE'S ASS by Stephen J. Glued

More philosophical musings on abstruse conundrums by the master of contemplative biology. Why do animals all have their heads in front and tails in back, when they would work just as well turned around? What developmental program enables legs and feet to grow just long enough to reach the ground, but no further? If evolution is based on "survival of the fittest," why, at this late date, are there so many jerks in the world?

THE HUNT FOR BLUE NOVEMBER by Tom Fancy

Submarine Captain Dorko Remus of the Former Soviet Navy and CIA hotshot hero Jack Cryan square off again to face a new challenge: How can they justify their continuing existence in the post–Cold War era? Whether trying to peddle PBS or BBC underwater documentaries, hijacking ocean liners and small pleasure yachts, or just shooting the bejesus out of flotsam and jetsam, Remus and Cryan are at their aquatic best. Fancy does it again!